EPILEPSY

Also by Tom McGowen

Chemistry:
The Birth of a Science

The Circulatory System:
From Harvey to the Artificial Heart

Midway and Guadalcanal

Radioactivity:
From the Curies to the Atomic Age

War Gaming

George Washington

TOM McGOWEN

EPILEPSY

Franklin Watts
New York / London / Toronto / Sydney / 1989
A Venture Book

Library of Congress Cataloging-in-Publication Data
McGowen, Tom.
Epilepsy.

(Venture)
Includes index.
Summary: Discusses the causes of epilepsy, how
it is diagnosed and treated, and what to do if someone
is having a seizure.
1. Epilepsy. [1. Epilepsy] I. Title.
RC372.M33   1989   616.8'53   89-5755
ISBN 0-531-10807-4

Dedicated to
every child who has epilepsy

Diagrams by: Anne Canevari Green

Photographs courtesy of:
New York Public Library Picture Collection:
pp. 15 (top left and right), 24, 26, 32;
Epilepsy Foundation of America:
p. 15 (bottom left and right);
Taurus Photos/Martin M. Rotker:
pp. 54, 55, 66 (both);
Photo Researchers: pp. 63 and 65
(Larry Mulvehill/Science Source),
78 (Robert Goldstein/Science Source);
Oxford Medical Inc.: p. 76

CONTENTS

Chapter One
What Is Epilepsy?
11

Chapter Two
Epilepsy in History
21

Chapter Three
What Makes an Epileptic Seizure Happen?
37

Chapter Four
What Causes Epilepsy?
51

Chapter Five
How Can Doctors Tell If a
Person Truly Has Epilepsy?
59

Chapter Six
How Do Doctors Treat Epilepsy?
69

Chapter Seven
What to Do If Someone You Know
Has an Epileptic Seizure
81

Glossary 85   Bibliography 89   Index 91

EPILEPSY

CHAPTER

1

WHAT IS EPILEPSY?

In a park in an American city, a group of boys are playing baseball. The twelve-year-old boy at bat stands in a half crouch, waving the bat menacingly, a determined look on his face. The pitcher, also twelve, stands facing him, looking equally determined. His teammates call out encouraging remarks—"Make him be a hitter!" "He can't hit; strike him out."

But suddenly the batter's body snaps upright and the bat drops from his hands. He utters a piercing shriek, then crumples to the ground. No one has pushed him, he didn't trip, he wasn't hit by a thrown ball, he isn't merely playing a trick; he has apparently just collapsed for no reason. He lies faceup with his eyes wide open and rolling. His arms and legs are jerking and twitching uncontrollably. The game comes to a halt as the other boys quickly gather around him. Frightened and uncertain, they wonder what has happened and what they should do.

After a few minutes the boy's body stops twitching and his eyes stop rolling. In a moment he weakly pushes himself up to a sitting position. With a grimace he puts a hand to his head, for he suddenly has a painful headache. His muscles feel stiff and sore.

At this same moment in another part of the city miles away, a six-year-old girl is eating her lunch, a bowl of soup. Between swallows she excitedly tells her mother about something she saw that morning.

But abruptly, an odd thing happens. As the girl is bringing the spoon toward her mouth she seems to suddenly "freeze." Her words stop dead in the middle of a sentence, her body becomes motionless, and she sits for several seconds with the spoon poised halfway to her mouth. Her eyes seem to be staring blankly at nothing.

Then, her gaze becomes alert once more. She begins talking again, at the exact point where she had stopped, and resumes moving the spoon toward her lips. She has no pain or discomfort, and she is completely unaware of what just happened to her.

In still another part of the city, a fourteen-year-old girl is walking vigorously down a street. Suddenly, she stops in her tracks. She has become aware of a tingling sensation in her right hand, and she knows what this means. She stands motionless for a time, a look of slight concern on her face. The tingling sensation moves up her arm to her shoulder, then it dies away and is gone. The girl gives a slight sigh of relief and begins to walk

(12)

again. Not much more than a minute has gone by since she first felt the tingling in her hand, and she was fully conscious and aware of what was happening all the time. Except for the tingling she felt perfectly normal, and now that the tingling is gone she feels fine.

All three of these young people, the twelve-year-old boy and the six- and fourteen-year-old girls, have the same kind of problem. They are all affected by the condition known as epilepsy, a name that comes from a Greek word that means "to seize." And all three youngsters have just been "seized," although they have each had a different kind of seizure, or attack, caused by their condition. What has happened is that, for several minutes for the boy and for just a few seconds for the girls, their brains simply stopped working properly, and this affected the rest of their bodies in a certain way.

Epilepsy is a condition that indicates a problem in the brain. At times there will be a kind of "electric storm" in the brain, and then the person will have a seizure. This may be nothing more than a period of a few seconds in which the person is simply unaware of what is going on around him or her. Or it may be a fainting spell in which the person is unconscious for as many as fifteen or twenty minutes, during which time his or her body, head, arms, and legs may violently twitch and jerk. An attack like this, which is what happened to the boy, may not happen to a person more than once or twice during a lifetime, or it may happen many times. An attack like the six-year-old girl's may happen as often as a hundred times during a day, or only a few times a month.

A third kind of attack resembles the one experienced by the fourteen-year-old girl. And there are still others: the victim may see, hear, or smell things that aren't really there, or may have a sudden vivid memory of a dream, or may suddenly begin to behave oddly, fumbling with clothing or repeatedly smacking the lips. Or a person's body or arms may suddenly jerk so violently that something he or she is holding will be hurled through the air. Or the victim thinks of the same word or group of words over and over, sometimes saying them aloud, again and again. Other attacks are nothing more than a twitching of a thumb or finger.

However, no one with epilepsy, no matter what kind of seizure experienced, is either "sick," diseased, or abnormal. Epilepsy is not a disease; it is a symptom of something wrong with a part of the body—the brain— just as deafness is generally a symptom of something wrong within the ears. Epilepsy is not contagious any more than deafness is contagious, and people with epilepsy are absolutely *not* "crazy," retarded, or mentally ill in any way. In fact, some of the most famous and accomplished people in history had epilepsy!

For example, Alexander the Great had it. He was king of Macedonia (a little country near ancient Greece) about twenty-three hundred years ago, and was also one of the greatest generals of history, who conquered the vast Persian Empire and became its ruler.

Julius Caesar had it. He was so famous and important that a month is named after him—July. He, too, was a great general, whose conquests some two thousand years ago formed the basis of the mighty Roman Empire.

Some of the most famous people in history had epilepsy. Top: Julius Caesar and George Frederick Handel; bottom: Vincent van Gogh and Napoleon Bonaparte.

George Frederick Handel had it. He was a famous composer of music who lived about three hundred years ago, and whose music is still played by symphony orchestras today. His famous work *Messiah* is played especially at Eastertime, all over the world.

Napoleon Bonaparte apparently had it. Another great general, Napoleon conquered most of Europe in the early 1800s and became emperor of the French First Empire. A system of law he created is still in use in France as are some of his policies on education and banking.

Vincent van Gogh, who lived a little more than a hundred years ago, had it. Today, he is regarded as one of the greatest of all artists, and his paintings are worth many millions of dollars—each!

Fyodor Dostoevski had it. A Russian writer who lived at about the same time as van Gogh, he wrote a number of novels that are considered to be classics, and have been translated into many languages and made into motion pictures in the twentieth century.

Obviously, having epilepsy didn't keep any of these men from doing things that made them some of the most famous persons in history. And there have been many other famous and accomplished men and women who had epilepsy—politicians, artists, writers, musicians, scientists, actors and actresses, and even athletes, such as the star baseball player Tony Lazzeri, who played with the New York Yankees, and the star hockey player Gary Howatt, of the New York Islanders. At least one pope—Pius IX—had epilepsy. Having epilepsy can be troublesome, annoying, and at times perhaps somewhat dangerous, but it is not a handicap.

Epilepsy is actually a fairly common condition. Some experts think that at least one person in every two hundred has it, and some doctors think the figure may be even higher—one person out of every hundred. But many people who have epilepsy do not even know it. They go through life unaware that the odd sensation or peculiar twitching of a thumb or finger that happens to them from time to time is actually an epileptic seizure.

Epilepsy isn't just a human problem; animals can have it, too. Epileptic seizures have been seen among cattle, certain types of mice, certain types of rabbits, and some other creatures. Of course, these animals belong to the same "family" humans belong to, the mammals, but scientists have found that epileptic seizures can be made to happen to other kinds of animals as well, such as frogs.

Apparently, any creature with a well-developed central nervous system can have an epileptic seizure.

About three-fourths of the people who have epilepsy have their first seizure before they are twenty years old. It usually happens between the ages of four and fourteen. Because of this, it was long believed that epilepsy was a disease of childhood that would generally show up by the time a person was a teenager, or else not at all. But actually, anyone can get epilepsy at any age. It can be brought on by a head injury; a brain tumor; a stroke; hardening of the arteries, a condition common among elderly people; and by a number of other things as well. No one is immune to epilepsy, no matter what age.

While most kinds of epilepsy are "harmless," in that they don't cause death or permanent brain disorder, it *is* possible to die from a condition known as *status epilepticus,* or "epileptic state." What happens in status epilepticus is that the person has a series of seizures, one after another, with no pause in between. Most often this condition, too, is harmless, with the person simply undergoing a steady jerking of one part of the body, such as a thumb or finger, for many hours, or else going into a kind of trance and staying dazed and sleepy for several days. But if the series of seizures is of the kind in which the person becomes unconscious and has a twitching and jerking of all parts of the body, there is grave danger. The longer these seizures keep happening, the higher the person's body temperature will climb, and in time the heart, lungs, and kidneys will stop working. Unless a person having such seizures is rushed to a hospital, where doctors can stop the seizures with medication, he or she is liable to die. Fortunately, status epilepticus seizures are fairly rare. For the most part they are caused when a person who has epilepsy suddenly stops taking epilepsy medication.

At the present time there is no cure for most kinds of epilepsy, although one kind, caused by a scar on the brain, can sometimes be cured with surgery. There are, however, medications of various kinds that can help control seizures. And because of the tremendous amount of research presently being done to learn more about how the brain works, and because of many promising discoveries constantly being made, there is definite hope that a way of preventing epilepsy will be found.

The main things to remember about epilepsy are these:

Epilepsy is not a disease and is not contagious in any way.

People with epilepsy are not retarded, mentally deficient, or "slow." Some of the brightest and most accomplished people in history had epilepsy. Many people who have epilepsy are quite able to drive cars, swim, travel, and do all the other things that people without epilepsy can do.

There are a number of different kinds of epileptic seizures. Some kinds are so slight that they aren't even noticeable.

No one is immune to epilepsy. Anyone can get it at any time in life, from a number of different causes.

People with epilepsy can live normal, useful, happy lives. There are many kinds of medications for preventing seizures, and many people who have epilepsy as children will actually "grow out of it" as they mature.

CHAPTER

2

EPILEPSY IN HISTORY

There have probably always been people troubled with epilepsy for as long as there have been people in the world. Our oldest record of epilepsy comes from the very dawn of history, when people first began to write down events and ideas. It is writing on a clay tablet that describes a person having an epileptic seizure, four thousand years ago. We can be sure, though, that people were having epileptic attacks even long before that, and that among our prehistoric ancestors, the people generally known as Cro-Magnons, there were individuals with epilepsy as far back as thirty thousand years ago. For that matter, it's very likely that some of our *very* distant ancestors, of many hundreds of thousands of years ago and more, were also affected by this disorder. So, for many thousands of years, epilepsy has affected millions of people from savages to scientists and from emperors to beggars. It is one of the oldest afflictions of the human race.

Epilepsy has been looked upon in many different ways throughout history. Four thousand years ago in the ancient Near East, people thought epileptic seizures were caused by evil spirits or demons that had gotten into a person's body, and priests attempted to cure people with epilepsy by driving the demons out of them with magic and prayers. So, in that time and place, epilepsy was believed to be caused by evil influences.

But in ancient Greece, around the time of Alexander the Great, twenty-three hundred years ago, epilepsy was known as "the sacred disease," because the Greeks believed that a person with epilepsy had been especially touched by the gods. Thus, for them, epilepsy was basically thought of as a divine, magical condition caused by good influences. To try to prevent seizures, priests and magicians suggested such remedies as having the person drink wine in which powdered human skull bone was mixed.

However, the ancient Greeks were the first people to come up with the basic idea of science, the idea of studying things to try to find out what made them happen rather than just believing that they happened from supernatural causes such as demons or gods. One of history's first and greatest doctors was a Greek known as Hippocrates, who was a true scientist, and it was Hippocrates who first figured out that epilepsy was a kind of disease rather than a magical condition caused by the gods, and he also decided that it was caused by a problem in the brain, which was absolutely right. Most other Greek doctors came to agree with Hippocrates, so eventually the idea that epilepsy was magical was replaced by the idea that it was simply another kind of illness like all the other illnesses that troubled people.

By the time of Julius Caesar of Rome, epilepsy had become known as "the falling sickness," because of those seizures that made a person lose consciousness and fall down. Doctors of Caesar's time, most of whom were Greeks, were all familiar with Hippocrates' diagnosis that epilepsy was a disease of the brain, but they had no idea how to cure it and thought up some odd remedies, such as putting blood on a person's lips. However, the greatest doctor of the Roman world, a man known as Galen, who lived in the second century A.D., worked out what was really a fairly sensible idea for the cause and treatment of epilepsy. He thought that the problem was probably caused by something blocking off the "passages" of the brain—probably a thick phlegm, such as a person with a chest cold coughs up. He suggested that people who had epilepsy should get plenty of exercise, follow a good diet, and make use of medicines that could "cut" and dissolve the phlegm. He was wrong about the cause of epilepsy of course, but at least his ideas were logical.

Galen was also the first doctor to learn that before some epileptic attacks begin, the person who is about to have the seizure has a kind of warning symptom. One of Galen's patients, a teenage boy, said that before his attacks began he always felt as if a cool breeze was moving up inside his body. Galen gave this symptom

In ancient Rome the great doctor
Galen had as his patient a teenage
boy with epilepsy. The boy told
Galen that just before a seizure
he always felt as if a cool breeze
was moving up inside his body.
Galen called this symptom an
aura, meaning "breeze."

the name *aura,* which is a Greek word meaning "breeze," and to this day doctors still use that name in the same way.

When the Roman Empire broke up in the fifth century A.D., most of its universities, libraries, and other institutions were destroyed or abandoned, and a great deal of knowledge was lost. Throughout most of Europe, for many hundreds of years, no one any longer knew, as the Greeks and Romans had, that epilepsy was a disorder of the brain. Instead, when someone had an epileptic seizure, people once again believed it was being caused by demons or evil influences. Martin Luther, the man who started the Protestant religious movement in the Middle Ages, called epilepsy "the demonic disease." Thus, persons known to have epilepsy were generally shunned and feared, because others were afraid they might get the "demonic disease" by associating with them or even by simply *looking* at them! It was believed that a person who had epilepsy could be "cleansed" only by having a saint drive out the demons in the body. One of the favorite saints for this sort of thing was Saint Valentine (whose feast day is still widely observed, as Valentine's Day), and it became common for sufferers to make a pilgrimage (journey) to the priory, or religious house, in western Germany where the saint was buried, in hope of being cured. Their "treatment" there consisted of attending three masses and then visiting the saint's grave.

Epilepsy was incorrectly considered to be contagious, and so afflicted people were often treated in much the same way as persons with the dreaded disease leprosy; they were isolated, or kept apart, from the rest of

(25)

Sixteenth-century Flemish painter Peter Breughel's drawing of persons with epilepsy dancing their way to a "healing well." Many superstitions surrounded epilepsy, and bizarre treatments were practiced.

the population. Special hospitals were built for them, in places such as the priory of St. Valentine, and there they had to stay for the rest of their lives. Some of these "hospitals" were actually prisons, and the "patients" were chained in their rooms or forced to wear shackles on their legs or wrists, so that they couldn't escape.

Doctors of this period of history, the Middle Ages, were divided in their opinion as to whether epilepsy was caused by demons that had entered a person's body or whether it was really just a disease. Those who were more inclined to think it was a disease tried to figure out what caused it, and many of them came to the conclusion that it was somehow caused by the moon, because it seemed to them that epileptic attacks occurred during the phases of the moon (that is, on nights when the moon was either one-quarter full, half-full, full, or dark). One doctor of the 1500s, a man known as Ferdinandus, traced a case of epilepsy back to the fact that the epileptic person had once spent an entire summer night out-of-doors, sleeping under an olive tree while the air was filled with "the slight warmth from the light of the moon."

Some doctors tried to cure epilepsy, but during the Middle Ages medical science was mostly a mixture of religion, magic, and folklore, and some of the remedies worked out for epilepsy seem quite weird to people of our own time. A famous English doctor of the 1300s suggested that someone with epilepsy might be cured by wearing garlands of peonies and chrysanthemums while listening to verses from the New Testament being read aloud. A French doctor of the 1500s suggested giving persons with epilepsy a concoction to eat made of mistletoe, powdered skull bone, and the seeds and roots of peony plants, gathered at night by the light of the moon.

Some doctors seemed to recognize that the cause of epilepsy was inside the brain, and so they directed their treatments at the heads of people with epilepsy. Such treatments were often drastic and painful. Iron rods, heated red hot in fire, were used to burn places on a person's skull, or in some cases a doctor would actually cut a hole into someone's skull in order to let out the "mischievous matter" that was causing the problem.

Doctors in parts of the world other than Europe were also doing what they could to treat epilepsy, and in some cases their treatments were far more sensible than those of the European doctors. In the Near East, Arab doctors of the Middle Ages often urged epileptic patients to eat as much fatty meat as possible, even to the point of making themselves feel nauseated. Actually, this *would* have been helpful to many persons with epilepsy, for today we know that eating a lot of fat produces certain chemicals in the bloodstream that help in preventing epileptic seizures. Apparently, the Arab doctors had discovered this in some way.

As time went on, new ideas and new discoveries began to emerge in Europe, and true science came into being. The use of magic and folklore began to decline, as did belief in supernatural causes, and scientists began to look for the natural causes of things. In the 1600s, Jan Marek, a Czechoslovakian doctor, discovered that certain occurrences, such as the sight of a flickering light, could often cause some persons with epilepsy to have seizures, and this was the beginning of a real understanding of what epilepsy actually is.

During the 1700s the movement known as the Enlightenment took place in Europe. This was a movement in which intelligent, educated people sought to get rid of superstition, prejudice, and many old-fashioned ideas of religion and politics. Most doctors completely stopped using any of the old magical folklore remedies for treating epilepsy and looked for remedies based on actual knowledge and common sense. A French doctor named Tissot, who was somewhat of a specialist on epilepsy, declared that the best medicine for those who had epilepsy was to simply try to stay healthy and avoid excitement, which was a far cry from giving them concoctions of powdered skull bone, blood, and other disgusting ingredients, as doctors of the Middle Ages had done. Thomas Beddoes, an English doctor of the 1700s, was one of the first to suggest that almost anyone could become afflicted with epilepsy. Many doctors of the 1700s were active in fighting to have the chains and shackles taken off epileptic and mental patients in mental institutions. So, in the 1700s conditions for people who had epilepsy began to improve somewhat for the first time in nearly two thousand years.

But while doctors and scientists were now doing their best to shed new light on epilepsy, a good many superstitions and folk beliefs still persisted among ordinary, uneducated people. In parts of Germany it was believed that if a baby under one year of age saw itself in a mirror it would have epilepsy when it grew up. Another common superstition was that the saliva (spit) of someone with epilepsy was poisonous. Most people believed that anyone with epilepsy was at least slightly "crazy," and many people, even some doctors, still believed that epilepsy was somehow caused by the moon and that seizures generally happened during the phases of the moon.

In 1854 a French doctor by the name of Moreau put an end to this old superstition. He kept a careful record of 42,637 epileptic seizures and was able to report that only 16,000 of them had happened during phases of the moon, while more than 26,000 had occurred *between* phases. This showed pretty conclusively that an epileptic seizure could happen at any time and the moon had nothing to do with it.

By the mid-1800s doctors had learned a great deal about the different kinds of epileptic seizures, but they still hadn't found a way of preventing or controlling seizures. Then, almost by accident, a great discovery was made.

On an evening in May 1857, there was a meeting of the Royal Medical and Chirurgical (surgical) Society of London, attended by many doctors. During the meeting one of the doctors, Sir Charles Locock, an obstetrician (a doctor who takes care of pregnant women and delivers their babies), happened to mention that he had given a substance known as bromide of potassium to about fifteen of his women patients who had frequent epileptic seizures, and the seizures had apparently been stopped for all but one of them. Bromide of potassium is a compound, or mixture, of the chemicals bromine and potassium, and for some time doctors had known that it had a soothing effect on people with nervous disorders, which was why Dr. Locock had thought it might help his epileptic women patients. However, it apparently hadn't occurred to Dr. Locock to see if this medication might help others who had epilepsy as well, but it did occur to some of the other doctors present. Dr. Samuel Wilks began trying bromide of potassium on all his epileptic patients, women and men, and found that it effectively stopped the seizures of most of them. So at last, after thousands of years, a remedy that really helped people with epilepsy had finally been found. It had to be administered carefully, because it often caused severe side effects, such as skin rashes, but many were willing to accept that in order to at last be free of their seizures.

In the late 1800s a number of doctors and medical scientists studied epilepsy and made new discoveries about it. One of these men was Dr. Hughlings Jackson, an Englishman, whose wife happened to have epilepsy. It was Dr. Jackson who first realized that an epileptic attack was caused by some sort of violent disturbance in the brain—as he put it, "an occasional sudden, massive, rapid and local discharge of the gray matter."

Despite such discoveries, treatment for epilepsy took a step backward for a while in the late nineteenth and early twentieth centuries. People with severe epilepsy were often forced to live in mental hospitals or special wards of ordinary hospitals where they were locked in. They were treated well enough, but this was still just like being in prison. They were also given frequent, extra-large doses of bromides, which, in many cases, apparently affected their personalities. Because of this, many doctors around the turn of the twentieth century believed that all persons with epilepsy had what is known

*In nineteenth-century America,
people with severe epilepsy
were sometimes confined
to lunatic asylums, where
they suffered maltreatment by
ill-trained asylum personnel.*

as "personality disorders"—that they were sly, irritable, likely to do sudden rash and foolish things, and so on.

However, in 1912 there was another major discovery that became of tremendous help in the treatment of epilepsy. A German doctor, Alfred Hauptmann, began to treat epileptic patients with the medication that is now known as phenobarbital or luminal. Dr. Hauptmann found that not only did this medication work better than bromides in helping prevent epileptic seizures, but that the general health and mental outlook of people taking it was far better than when they had been taking bromides. Thus, the use of phenobarbital helped wipe away the idea that people with epilepsy had personality disorders. In time, most patients with epilepsy were released from mental hospitals and prisonlike wards, and the practice of keeping them apart from other people came to an end.

In the late 1920s there was an invention that was to become a major tool in diagnosing epilepsy. An Austrian, Dr. Johannes Berger, perfected the machine that became known as the electroencephalograph. With this machine, which could record the electrical activity of a person's brain, doctors could actually *see* the abnormal activity of the brain of a person with epilepsy.

By this time, with all that was known about epilepsy, all the old-fashioned ideas and superstitions should have been laid to rest. But unfortunately, they weren't—there were even some new ones. Some people still believed that epilepsy was somehow contagious, and many still believed that sufferers were mentally impaired and might become dangerous. An idea had arisen that epilepsy caused people to become criminals, and that many afflicted people committed crimes either during or just after an epileptic seizure. And it was generally believed that epilepsy was hereditary—that is, that an epileptic parent would pass epilepsy along to his or her children. Because of all such ideas, life was still full of difficulties for those with epilepsy, up until very recently. For example, up until the 1970s it was against the law in many parts of the United States for any person with epilepsy to get married! This was because it was believed that such persons would pass the condition along to their children, who then might have to be kept in an institution at government expense. The last law of this sort was abolished only in 1982.

Some difficulties and unfair practices still exist. In most cases a person with epilepsy has to pay a higher amount for life insurance than other people do. It is difficult for many people with epilepsy to get a driver's license, and for those who can, it is usually difficult and costly to get automobile insurance. It is hard for some to get a hunting or fishing license, because of the fear that they might be drowned or injured during a seizure. And in some cases it may not be easy to get a job, because some employers are afraid to take a chance on hiring anyone with epilepsy.

There are also still many people who don't know anything about epilepsy and believe some of the ancient folklore and superstition about it. But as new medications are created that can finally control seizures with absolute certainty, and as people become better educated about what epilepsy actually is, it can be hoped that the day will soon come when someone with epilepsy isn't regarded any differently from, for example, a person with an annoying chronic allergy such as hay fever—someone to be mildly sympathized with, but not in the least bit feared or restricted.

CHAPTER

3

WHAT MAKES AN EPILEPTIC SEIZURE HAPPEN?

An epileptic seizure takes place when the normal working of the brain is suddenly interrupted.

The brain is the body's control center. Although it is an extremely complicated organ it looks merely like a melon-shaped, grayish-pink lump, creased with many deep folds, like crevices. Like all the other parts of the body it is formed of many billions of microscopic living structures that we call cells. Throughout the body there are different kinds of cells that do different kinds of jobs, and the brain has two kinds—*neurons,* or nerve cells, which handle information, and *glia,* which act as a kind of "support force" for the neurons, keeping them healthy and protected. Most of the outer surface of the brain is composed of a layer of neurons, about ⅛ of an inch (0.3 cm) thick, which has a grayish color and is

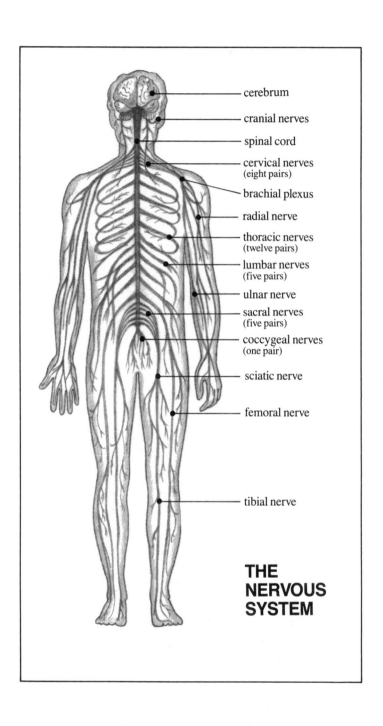

cerebrum

cranial nerves

spinal cord

cervical nerves
(eight pairs)

brachial plexus

radial nerve

thoracic nerves
(twelve pairs)

lumbar nerves
(five pairs)

ulnar nerve

sacral nerves
(five pairs)

coccygeal nerves
(one pair)

sciatic nerve

femoral nerve

tibial nerve

THE NERVOUS SYSTEM

often referred to as "gray matter." The folds in the brain's surface increase the surface much more than if it were completely smooth, and this provides more room for neurons—in other words, if you could unfold a human brain until it was a flat sheet, it would have a much greater area than a smooth object of the same size would have if it were unfolded the same way. Animals have smoother brains and therefore less surface area and less gray matter, and this is why humans are smarter.

The brain is composed of three basic parts:

1. A large upper portion called the cerebrum (a Latin word meaning simply "brain"), which makes up about 85 percent of the whole brain;
2. An orange-size part called the cerebellum (another Latin word, meaning "rear brain"), which is beneath and to the rear of the cerebrum;
3. A stalklike part called the brain stem, that connects to the spinal cord.

Running about two-thirds down the back, inside the backbone, the spinal cord contains "pathways" that carry information from all parts of the body to the brain, and from the brain to all parts of the body.

Throughout the body there are special kinds of neurons, or nerve cells, called receptors (receivers). They have the job of turning information coming into the body in the form of sight, sound, taste, smell, and feel, into messages that are sent to the brain. These messages, or impulses, go racing along paths formed by chains of nerve cells, traveling at tremendous speeds and reaching the brain in only a tiny fraction of a second. Thus, from the eyes, nose, ears, skin, and other body parts, the brain constantly receives a steady flow of information about what is going on outside and inside the body. Within the brain, clusters of special cells that act much like computers take in this information, analyze it, and "decide" whether to send a message back through the body's nervous system to a muscle, gland, or other body part telling it to do, or not to do, something. This, too, takes only a tiny fraction of a second, and is going on constantly, day and night, whether the body is awake or asleep.

Thus, the brain is in control of all functions, or working, of the body. Different parts of the brain control different functions. The cerebrum is divided, by a deep groove, into two equal halves, and the left half, in general, controls the body's ability to speak and understand, while the right half controls the ability to understand what the eyes see, and to express emotion. The cerebellum controls the ability to move about without bumping into things or lurching or stumbling, the ability to pick up things, etc. Each half of the cerebrum is divided into four regions known as lobes, and these lobes handle sight, hearing, smell, taste, and touch. An area called the motor cortex controls the body's muscles. Damage to any of these control areas can cause loss or impairment of the functions they control.

A neuron, or nerve cell, of the brain, which sends and receives messages, faintly resembles a tree with a long trunk having a swollen area at its top, out of which many thin branches spread. The "trunk" is called an *axon*, which basically means "straight line," and the "branches" are called *dendrites*, from a Greek word meaning "tree." A neuron has around twenty thousand

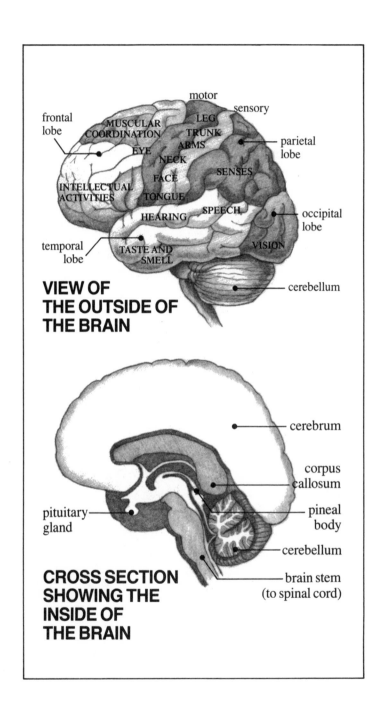

motor

sensory

frontal lobe

MUSCULAR COORDINATION

LEG
TRUNK
ARMS

EYE

NECK

parietal lobe

FACE

SENSES

INTELLECTUAL ACTIVITIES

TONGUE

HEARING

SPEECH

occipital lobe

temporal lobe

TASTE AND SMELL

VISION

cerebellum

**VIEW OF
THE OUTSIDE OF
THE BRAIN**

cerebrum

corpus callosum

pituitary gland

pineal body

cerebellum

brain stem
(to spinal cord)

**CROSS SECTION
SHOWING THE
INSIDE OF
THE BRAIN**

dendrites branching out of the swollen area at the top of the axon. This swollen area is actually the main part of the cell, containing the *nucleus,* a Latin word meaning "seed," a complicated arrangement of chemical substances that the cell uses to keep itself in good working order. Neurons are not connected to one another, but they can transmit impulses to one another, with the impulse traveling down the axon of one neuron and into a dendrite of another neuron. Chemistry and electricity cause this to happen. A chemical reaction takes place in one part of a neuron, which produces an electric charge that starts a chemical reaction in the next closest part, producing another electric charge. Eventually, within a tiny fraction of a second, an electric charge jumps to the next neuron, setting up a chemical reaction that triggers the same process in it. Thus, a series of impulses can flash along a path of neurons to a particular part of the body, telling it to do something.

Neurons are arranged in groups of hundreds of thousands, and for most people the neurons in any one group are all doing different things at the same time. Some will be generating chemical reactions, some generating electric charges, some doing nothing at all for a moment. But in the brains of people who have epilepsy there is sometimes a misfiring of a group of neurons, and they all discharge electric impulses at the same time. This generally creates enough activity to trigger electric discharges in nearby groups of neurons so that large areas of neurons are suddenly "going off" all together. This can shut down or throw out of kilter parts of the brain that control various functions of the body, and this is what causes an epileptic seizure.

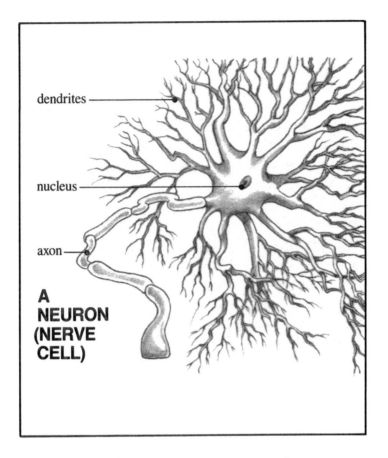

dendrites

nucleus

axon

A NEURON (NERVE CELL)

Normally a neuron transmits an electric charge to the neuron closest to it, which then transmits the charge to the next neuron in the group. This series of impulses carries messages to various parts of the body. In the brains of people who have epilepsy there is sometimes a misfiring, so that all the neurons within a group may discharge electric impulses at the same time.

There are different kinds of seizures depending upon the part of the brain being affected by the misfiring neurons. The most common type, which affects more than half of all people with epilepsy, is known as a *grand mal,* or "great sickness," seizure. In a grand mal seizure the discharge of neurons spreads across both halves of the brain, cutting off the "awareness" and "understanding" portions of the brain so that the person suddenly loses consciousness. Messages to the body's muscles are temporarily cut off, and the person's muscles become rigid, the whole body stiff.

The sudden stiffening of the chest muscles pushes all the air out of the person's lungs, causing a whistling sound or high-pitched shriek. And the stiffness of the body's other muscles, together with the loss of awareness, causes the person to fall to the ground. Because there is no air in the lungs, the skin may take on a bluish tinge, which indicates lack of oxygen in the blood.

But now, nerve impulses are beginning to get through again, and the rigid body starts to relax, letting air rush back into the lungs. Gradually the body loses all its stiffness, but because the motor cortex has been affected the person's head, torso, arms, and legs begin to jerk, rapidly and evenly, or *rhythmically.* As time passes and the motor cortex regains control, the jerking becomes more uneven and less rapid. After five or ten minutes the jerking generally stops altogether.

During all this time, some persons bite their tongue or lose control of their bowels or bladder. Air mixed with saliva in the mouth causes a white froth around the lips so that the person often appears to be foaming at the mouth. After the jerking of the body parts stops, the person generally remains unconscious for a few more minutes. When he or she comes to, the person is generally confused and weak, with a headache and stiff, sore muscles, and may be very sleepy.

Doctors call this type of a seizure a *tonic-clonic seizure*. *Tonic* comes from a Greek word meaning "stiffness," and the first part of a tonic-clonic seizure is, of course, stiffness of the whole body. *Clonic*, from a Greek word meaning "violent action," refers to the violent jerking of the body parts during the seizure.

However, the discharge of neurons across both halves of the brain does not always result in a tonic-clonic seizure. For many people it causes what is known as a *petit mal*, or "little sickness," seizure, which doctors more commonly call an *absence seizure*. An absence seizure strikes without warning, and, as in the case of a tonic-clonic seizure, the person loses consciousness, but only for a period of from about five to thirty seconds. The person appears to be staring blankly as if deep in thought or daydreaming. The eyes stay open and may seem to roll back slightly into the head, and there may be slight, rhythmic twitches of facial muscles or of the head or arms. If talking or moving when the seizure began, the person may stop suddenly in the middle of a sentence or "freeze" in the middle of a movement. Then, abruptly, the seizure ends and the person becomes fully conscious again and continues whatever he or she has been doing, without even being aware that anything happened.

And there are still other types of seizures caused by the discharge of neurons across both halves of the cerebrum. In one of these, called an *atonic,* or "drop," seizure, the person doesn't lose consciousness but simply loses control of the muscles and falls to the ground. But he or she is able to get up again right away, and there are no aftereffects. In another type of attack, called a *myoclonic* ("violent action of muscle") seizure, the person has such violent muscle jerks that he or she is often hurled to the ground. In general, these two kinds of seizures are much more rare than tonic-clonic or absence seizures.

A completely different form of seizure is caused when the electric discharge of neurons affects only one side of the brain. The person having the seizure does not lose consciousness, but has problems with awareness, sensations, or movement, depending upon the areas of the brain being affected. This kind of seizure generally begins with a dreamy feeling, as if the person is dreaming rather than awake. Things look odd and "different" and there is a feeling of strangeness. The person may smell a particular smell of something that isn't actually there—generally a strong, sharp smell—or may suddenly have a strong taste in the mouth—a bitter, sour, or very sweet taste. This is because the brain's temporal lobes, where taste and smell are controlled, are being affected by the neuron discharge. Persons having this kind of seizure often wander about aimlessly and perform such old actions as plucking at their clothing or repeatedly smacking their lips. A seizure of this sort is generally known as a *psychomotor* ("mind-action") *seizure*, because it affects both awareness and activity. A psychomotor seizure usually lasts only three or four minutes, leaving the person who had it confused and disoriented and unaware of what happened. At times, however, a psychomotor seizure will turn into a tonic-clonic seizure because the neuron discharge spreads from one half of the brain to the other.

Neuron misfirings in particular parts of the brain cause still other types of seizures. What is called a *motor seizure* travels along the surface of the front part of the brain, affecting neurons that control different muscles. The seizure may begin with a strong tingling in the fingers of one hand, which moves up the arm and then perhaps down a leg, on one side of the body only. Generally the person will not lose consciousness unless the neuron discharge spreads. A *sensory seizure,* affecting the optical cortex which controls vision, may cause a person to see things such as whirling or flashing lights, bursts of color, or geometric shapes. When the auditory cortex, which handles hearing, is affected, the person may hear a steady humming, buzzing, or hissing sound, or perhaps normal sounds will suddenly seem louder or softer than usual. Of course, none of these things is actually happening in the eyes or ears; they are happening in the brain.

Still another kind of seizure that affects only a part of the brain is the *autonomic seizure,* affecting the autonomic nervous system, which controls such things as heartbeat and digestion. The affected person may have a series of severe headaches, or stomachaches, or an upset stomach with vomiting, or a fever. None of these things seems much like any other kind of epileptic seizure, and all of them can easily be mistaken for symptoms of a number of different diseases, so a doctor may not discover that they're being caused by epilepsy until other possibilities have been ruled out.

Tonic-clonic, absence, and other seizures caused by neurons misfiring over the whole brain are called "general seizures," whereas psychomotor, motor, and sensory seizures are called "partial seizures" because neurons are misfiring only in parts of the brain. But what is it that causes neurons to misbehave as they do and spark all these kinds of seizures? The basic cause, of course, is that a person has something wrong in the brain that allows the neurons to do this, but there are apparently a number of things that can set the neurons off and cause an attack. Not getting enough sleep for too long a time can apparently cause some persons with epilepsy to have seizures. An infection in some part of the body may cause a seizure in some cases of epilepsy. The overuse of certain kinds of medicines, such as cold remedies or sleeping pills, seems to cause seizures for some people. Thus, it is important for people who have epilepsy to pay special attention to their health and hygiene.

But for some, seizures can be caused by simple, everyday things that have no effect on other people. A flashing light, such as an advertising sign; a faulty traffic signal that blinks over and over, or even a flickering TV screen; too long a look at a repetitive pattern, such as a checkerboard; or listening to a strain of music repeated over and over—any of these things may cause a seizure in some people with epilepsy, and so they must be constantly on guard.

Most afflicted people have only one kind of epilepsy and one kind of seizure. But there are some who may have two or even three different kinds of seizures during their lifetime. And sometimes a person who has had only one kind of seizure for many years will suddenly begin to have another kind from then on. Quite often a person who has only absence seizures as a child will begin having tonic-clonic or psychomotor seizures instead in adulthood.

It might seem as if having an epileptic seizure would cause a certain amount of brain damage, and that the more seizures people with epilepsy had, the more brain damage they might suffer, causing their intelligence to become impaired. At one time, doctors thought this was the case, but now we know that it isn't. Some time ago, a doctor kept records of a number of pairs of twins, each pair consisting of one twin who had epilepsy and one who didn't. Periodically, he checked the intelligence level of every twin. He found that the intelligence of the twins who had epileptic seizures did not drop in comparison with that of their brothers and sisters who had no seizures. Having epileptic seizures does not impair intelligence, cause mental retardation, or any such thing.

CHAPTER

4

WHAT CAUSES
EPILEPSY?

In general, doctors think of epilepsy in two ways. If they are able to find out what it is that has caused a person to have epilepsy they say that the person has "symptomatic epilepsy." *Symptomatic* means "a sign, or indication." If doctors can't tell what is causing the epilepsy in a person, they call it "idiopathic epilepsy," with the word *idiopathic* meaning a condition that is not caused by anything else.

About one-third of all persons with epilepsy have symptomatic epilepsy—doctors are able to determine what is causing it. For the most part, the cause of symptomatic epilepsy is something that has done serious damage to the brain or nervous system at some time during the person's life.

Around 43 percent of all cases of symptomatic epilepsy are caused by an injury to a baby's brain before birth or while it is being born. This can happen in a number of ways. If a mother catches an infectious (contagious) disease, such as German measles, while the baby is forming inside her body, the baby's brain can be damaged. If a mother should take a poisonous substance, such as most kinds of drugs, this can cause damage to the brain of the baby forming inside her. If she should be exposed to radiation, such as atomic radiation or even large amounts of X rays, there can be damage to her unborn baby's brain. And while a baby is being born, if something happens to keep it from getting enough oxygen for a time, its brain can be damaged. For example, a baby inside a mother's body is connected to her by a long tube, and sometimes this tube becomes wrapped around the baby's neck as it is coming out of the mother's body, cutting off its air.

Some 27 percent of cases of symptomatic epilepsy are caused by a person having an infectious disease during childhood. Certain diseases caused by viruses and bacteria can cause damage to the brain, resulting in epilepsy. With the disease called meningitis, which is an inflammation of the material that surrounds and protects the brain, there is danger that the virus causing the inflammation may actually move into the brain, causing damage. Tuberculosis, a disease that most often causes damage to the lungs, can result in damage to the brain if the bacteria causing it are able to spread from the lungs to the brain. Even measles, a very common and usually mild disease, can cause damage to the brain under certain conditions.

About 17 percent of symptomatic epilepsy is caused by a head injury at some time during a person's life. A hard blow to the head caused by a bad fall or an automobile accident or a thrown object, may fracture the skull and push a fragment of bone into the brain. Even a less serious injury can tear blood vessels, causing a blood clot to form that will put pressure on the brain. Experts have estimated that there are many thousands of cases of epilepsy created every year as a result of head injuries, chiefly caused by automobile accidents.

A brain tumor can do serious damage to the brain and cause epilepsy. A brain tumor is a lump on the brain, inside the skull, caused by the abnormal growth of a number of certain kind of cells that form the tissue, or material, covering the surface of the brain. Brain tumors can sometimes cause death, but in many cases a tumor can be successfully removed by surgery and the person who had the tumor can live on to a ripe old age. However, about one-third of the time the damage that has been done to the brain by the tumor will result in epilepsy. Epilepsy caused by a brain tumor is the most common kind of epilepsy in older people past the age of fifty.

Another cause of epilepsy in older people is a condition known as "hardening of the arteries," or *arteriosclerosis*. In this condition, the arteries, which are tubes that carry blood from the heart to all parts of the body, become slowly filled up with a substance, either chalk-like calcium or fatty cholesterol, that makes them harder and thicker until there is hardly enough space for the blood to flow through. Of course, pressure builds up as the blood tries to push its way through the narrowest

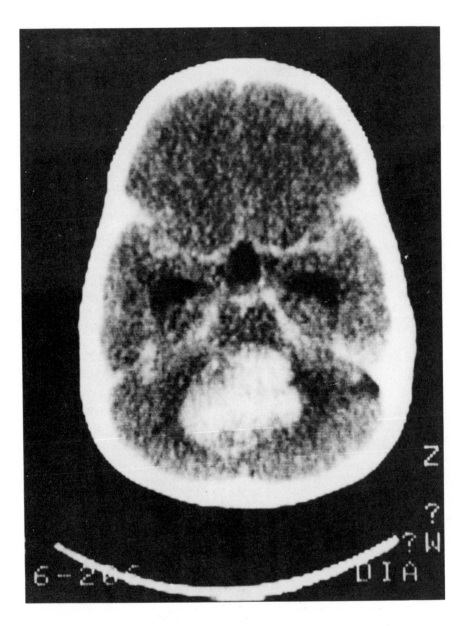

A CAT scan of a human brain.
The white mass is a tumor.

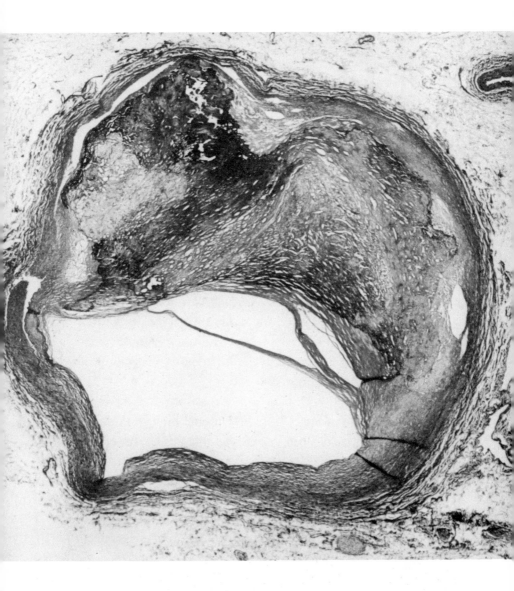

*A highly magnified photograph
of a coronary artery afflicted
with arteriosclerosis, often the
cause of epilepsy in older people.*

places, and this may cause an artery to rupture, or burst. When this happens in the artery that leads into the brain, a "stroke" occurs—blood leaks out into the brain and there is damage to the area, which can later cause epilepsy.

Brain damage can apparently also be caused by certain chemical disturbances in the body, such as when the amount of sodium or sugar in the body drops too low as a result of certain diseases. And a bad case of accidental poisoning by certain chemical substances may also affect the brain—for example, if a very young child should eat chips or flakes of dry paint that contains lead, brain damage can result.

It is easy to see that *anyone* can become afflicted with symptomatic epilepsy at any time in life as a result of a number of causes. A serious illness that affects the brain, such as encephalitis or meningitis, a severe head injury, a brain tumor, the use of poisonous substances such as drugs, and, later in life, hardening of the arteries and strokes can all produce a condition in the brain that will leave it open to epileptic seizures of some kind. The seizures may begin within a few months or they may not occur for as many as forty years, but once the damage that produces epilepsy has been done, the possibility of a seizure of some kind is always present.

The reason that all these things, such as head injuries, certain diseases, and so on, cause epilepsy is that in most cases they leave a scar of some sort on the brain, and it seems that epileptic seizures often begin in the area of such scars. Doctors can detect a scar on a brain in a number of ways and can thus tell that a person has symptomatic epilepsy. However, even when doctors know for sure that epilepsy is being caused by a scar on the brain, they still don't know exactly *why* a scar should cause such a problem. There are a number of ideas, but the one that many doctors suspect is most likely is that a scar may cause many of the neurons around it to become "supersensitive," and if something happens to make these supersensitive neurons start getting a lot of signals (something such as intense excitement, fear, or stress), they go out of control and all start discharging at the same time. But it is not *definitely* known that this is what happens.

About two-thirds of all cases of epilepsy are idiopathic rather than symptomatic; that is, doctors simply can't tell what causes them. The people with idiopathic epilepsy may never have had any serious infectious diseases in childhood, nor a head injury, nor any of the other things that can cause symptomatic epilepsy. In most cases, idiopathic epilepsy appears in a person before the age of twenty and has no known cause.

But here, too, doctors have some ideas as to why epileptic seizures may happen to people with idiopathic epilepsy. Neurons manufacture chemical substances within themselves which are used in the neuron's work of sending and receiving impulses. Perhaps if not enough, or too much, of this substance is made, the neuron becomes unable to work properly. If this should happen to a number of neurons all at once, it might cause the discharges that start a brain "storm."

Again, though, as to *why* this should happen—*why* a neuron should produce too much or too little of its chemicals—there is no answer. Many doctors seem to feel that persons with idiopathic epilepsy were simply born with certain defects in the way their brain and body work that makes them susceptible to epileptic seizures. This doesn't mean that epilepsy is actually hereditary, or passed along from a parent to a child. But it does mean that certain genes—the tiny units that control chemical processes in a cell, and that *are* passed along from a parent to a child—may have a defect that, in combination with other conditions in a person's body, can cause the person to become susceptible to epileptic seizures. A great deal more study needs to be done to find out about this and to discover what the cause or causes of idiopathic epilepsy may be.

CHAPTER

5

HOW CAN DOCTORS TELL IF A PERSON TRULY HAS EPILEPSY?

If a mother and father see their child suddenly have what seems to be an epileptic seizure they are sure to be shocked and frightened and want to quickly find out if the child has epilepsy. If an adult suddenly begins having fainting spells or begins to see, hear, or smell things that aren't really there, he or she is bound to be worried and want to find out what is going wrong. But there are a number of diseases and conditions that can cause people, especially young children, to have seizures similar to epileptic seizures. Therefore, doctors generally have to determine whether it was one of these ailments or epilepsy itself that caused the apparent seizure.

Sometimes when a baby or a young child of two or three is doing a lot of hard crying, he or she will run completely out of breath after letting out a long wail, and may actually stop breathing. Small children who are having temper tantrums will sometimes deliberately hold their breath. In either case, if the child goes for too long a time before taking a breath, it may faint because its body is deprived of oxygen, which is needed to keep the brain working as well as for a good many other things, and which can only be brought into the body by breathing. At times, such a fainting spell will look like an epileptic seizure—the child's arms and legs may twitch and it may lose control of its bladder, because its brain processes are affected by the lack of oxygen. A spell of this sort is generally over in about ten or fifteen seconds, because once the child is unconscious it automatically starts to breath again, and with oxygen once more in its body it will come to. But parents who have seen their child lying unconscious with twitching arms and legs may well think the child has had an epileptic attack.

Young children seem to catch colds, flu, and viral infections very easily, and will often run a very high fever with such illnesses. This can sometimes cause them to go into convulsions—a twitching and jerking of the limbs and body—that look like an epileptic seizure.

Among older people, as well as children, there are certain ailments that can act like epilepsy. A condition known as *hypoglycemia,* which causes the amount of sugar in a person's body to drop very low, can cause fainting spells and confused thoughts, much like some kinds of epileptic seizures. Heart trouble can sometimes cause symptoms that might also be caused by epilepsy, as can a brain tumor. And there are other things as well.

Because of all this, when a person has a seizure of some sort, the first thing a doctor wants to find out is whether the seizure was truly caused by epilepsy or by something else. The doctor will generally begin by trying to find out exactly how the seizure affected the person, and does this simply by asking questions. Before the seizure began did the patient feel peculiar in any way—perhaps as if a cool breeze was flowing through the body? If the answer is yes, the doctor knows that the person experienced an aura, which is a typical symptom of an epileptic attack. Was the patient looking at anything in particular before the seizure began, such as a flashing or flickering light, or a checkerboard? Again, a yes answer is a good indication that the person has the kind of epilepsy in which attacks are triggered by such things. Did the seizure affect both sides of the body or one side only? If only one side was affected, this is an indication that the seizure was caused by one form of epilepsy.

If the patient is a very young child, or if the seizure led to unconsciousness so that the patient doesn't know everything that happened, the doctor will try to find out how the patient acted from parents, family members, or friends who were present during the seizure. The doctor will also ask questions about the patient's general health, and about his or her behavior and attitudes. The answer to these questions can often go a long way toward indicating whether the seizure was epileptic or not.

The doctor will also give the patient a physical examination: measuring the patient's pulse and blood pressure; listening to the sounds of the heart and lungs;

checking the eyes with an opthalmoscope; testing the body's reflexes by tapping the knees with a hammer to see if the legs jerk upward as they should; stroking the underside of the foot to see which way the toes curl; and having the patient walk a straight line, placing one foot in front of the other. This general physical examination, too, may help reveal whether the patient's seizure was caused by epilepsy or something else.

But the questioning and the physical examination may not reveal enough, so the doctor may want to make a number of tests that can either rule out or prove certain things. An examination of a person's blood, looked at through a microscope and given certain chemical tests, can show if a person has hypoglycemia. An *electrocardiogram,* in which the rhythm of the heartbeat is electrically charted, can show if a person has a heart problem. A test of a small amount of fluid from a person's spinal column will show if meningitis bacteria are present.

To check for the possibility of a brain tumor or stroke, a patient may be given what is called a *CAT scan.* This is an examination by a machine that shoots a thin stream of X rays through the brain and, with the information this provides, uses a computer to produce pictures of segments, or "slices," of the brain. (CAT stands for computer-assisted tomography, and tomograph means "section picture.") For such an examination, a person lies flat on a bedlike, wheeled table with his or her head inside an opening in the machine. There is no pain or discomfort, and the pictures of the person's brain that are produced will show if there is a tumor, an abscess, or damage caused by a stroke.

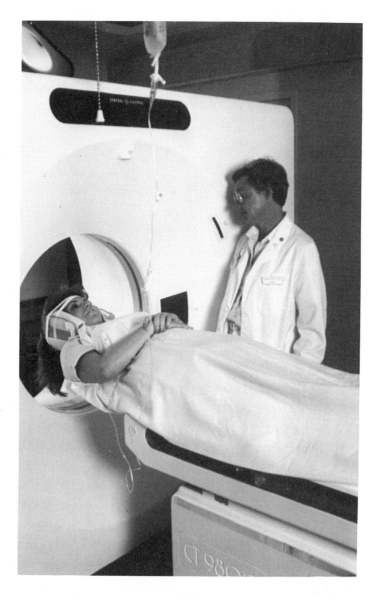

This woman is being given a CAT scan, a painless, nonsurgical method of examining the brain.

Once a doctor, by means of such tests, has ruled out the possibility of most ailments other than epilepsy, a test will generally be made to try to definitely establish that the patient's seizure or seizures were caused by epilepsy. The best tool that doctors have for this at present is a machine called an electroencephalograph, which literally means "a picture of the electrical activity of the brain."

In an examination by an electroencephalograph, little metal disks or needlelike rods, attached to the machine by wires, are placed on several parts of a person's head. When the machine is turned on, these metal disks or needles, called electrodes, can pick up the electric impulses that are being given off by the person's brain. The impulses travel along the wires into movable metal "arms" that function as pens, causing them to move up and down according to the strength of the impulses, making a steady pattern on a long sheet of paper that rolls along beneath them. The pattern produced on the long roll of paper shows the form, voltage, and frequency of the brain's electric impulses. For most people who have no problem in the brain, the pattern on the paper is simply rows of long wiggly lines, but for persons with epilepsy a distinctly different pattern is generally formed—about two-thirds of the way along the wiggly lines the wiggles suddenly become a series of sharp, jagged spikes followed by deep waves.

This picture of brain waves is called an electroencephalogram (EEG), and in most cases an electroencephalogram will show that a person who has had epileptic-like seizures does, indeed, have epilepsy. But not always. In about ten cases out of every hundred, a person who actually has epilepsy will nevertheless have a

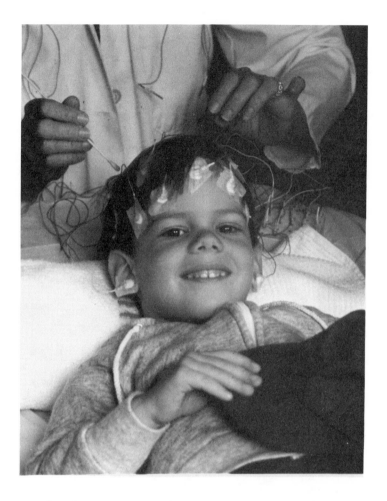

*Another nonsurgical way to examine the brain
is by the means of an electroencephalograph.
Here, metal disks, called electrodes, are being
placed at various spots on a young patient's
head. These electrodes will convey electric
impulses from the patient's brain to movable
metal "arms" that will record the impulses
on a long sheet of paper. This visual record
is called an electroencephalogram, or EEG.*

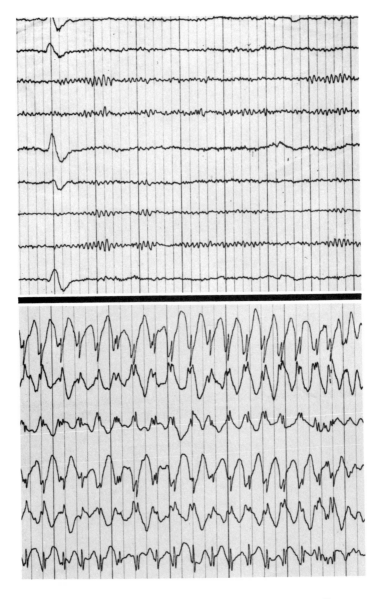

Top: *an EEG of a brain functioning normally.*
Bottom: *an EEG recording an epileptic*
seizure. Compare the pattern of sharp peaks and
valleys with the more linear pattern above.

normal-appearing electroencephalogram, while some people who have never had any kind of seizure at all will produce an electroencephalogram that has a spike-and-wave pattern.

But, all in all, by means of questions, a physical examination, tests for other ailments, and the use of the electroencephalograph, a doctor is almost always able to gather enough information to determine positively whether a person has epilepsy. Then the doctor can begin the kind of treatment needed to keep the patient's epileptic seizures under control and to help him or her lead a normal or nearly normal life.

CHAPTER

6

HOW DO DOCTORS TREAT EPILEPSY?

People with epilepsy are far better off today than at any other time in history. Not only do doctors know much more about the condition, but there are also medications available, known as anticonvulsant drugs, which in many cases can either prevent a person with epilepsy from ever having a seizure or at least make a person's seizures far fewer than they otherwise would be.

Most of these medications are in the form of a tablet, a capsule, or a liquid. These medications are swallowed and go into the stomach, where they are dissolved by the stomach's digestive fluids, becoming molecules (microscopic clusters) of chemicals. These are carried down into the intestines where they pass through the intestinal walls into the bloodstream, which carries them through the body and eventually into the brain.

There, in some way that still isn't fully understood, they actually "calm down," or suppress, the neurons that are most likely to start firing all at once and cause a seizure. Because the chemicals are in solution in the bloodstream they are spread out, like paint poured into a river, so they don't all reach the brain at once, but rather a little at a time, slowly and steadily, over several hours. They don't stay in the brain, but are carried on along through the body by the blood until they reach the liver. One of the jobs that the liver does is to get rid of any "alien" substances that get into the body, and as far as the liver is concerned, the chemicals of an anticonvulsant drug are alien substances, so it breaks them up and sends them to the bladder. There, they are mixed with water and eventually flushed out of the body by means of urination. By that time it will be necessary for the person to take another pill, capsule, or dose of liquid, in order to keep a continuous supply of the neuron-calming chemicals flowing to the brain.

There are a number of anticonvulsant medications, with such names as Dilantin, Zarontin, and Depakene. Most of these work better against one kind of epilepsy than another. Dilantin is, at present, one of the best medications for preventing tonic-clonic seizures, but it is useless against petit mal, or absence, seizures. Zarontin is quite effective against petit mal, but of no value against tonic-clonic seizures. So, obviously, the doctor has to pick the medication that will work best for the patient's particular condition.

But choosing the right drug is only part of the doctor's responsibilities. The doctor also has to determine exactly how large a dose of any medication is needed to give the patient the best protection against seizures. Too low a dose may not prevent seizures well enough, but the higher the dose the greater the danger there is that the patient may begin to suffer from side effects, for unfortunately, all the anticonvulsant drugs now available can cause different kinds of unpleasant and even harmful side effects to many people. For example, Dilantin causes the gums of most patients to become soft and puffy and to bleed easily. Depakene may cause drowsiness, nausea, an unpleasant-feeling dryness of the mouth, and itchy skin rashes. Zarontin can cause nausea and vomiting, as well as drowsiness and skin rashes.

So, the doctor has to first see if the prescribed dosage is working well enough for the patient. If the seizures seem to be well under control and there are no side effects from the medication, then all is well and the patient simply keeps on with that dosage. But if there are problems, the doctor will have to examine a sample of the patient's blood to determine the amount of the medication that the dosage is putting into the patient's bloodstream, and will then raise or lower the dosage accordingly; raising it if control of the seizures is not effective, and lowering it slightly if it is causing bad side effects. The goal is to try to achieve a balance between a dosage that's high enough to control the seizures and low enough not to cause side effects.

It may often be necessary to switch the patient from one medication to another, because the first medication doesn't work well enough or because it causes side effects that a patient just can't live with. For example, one of the relatively harmless side effects of Dilantin is that it can cause facial hair to grow more vigorously on some people. If the patient taking Dilantin is a young girl or woman who is suddenly horrified to see that she is growing a faint moustache, the doctor will most probably switch her to another medication, such as Depakene, which is a fairly good control for tonic-clonic seizures and does not cause hair to grow.

In many cases however, patients will simply learn to live with the side effects of the medication they are taking, as long as it helps control their seizures. Patients with tonic-clonic seizures who are taking Dilantin and who become afflicted with puffy, bleeding gums as a result, generally just maintain a program of good dental hygiene, with regular visits to a dentist, to keep the gum problem under as much control as possible. They don't mind having a minor problem with their gums as long as their medication is preventing them from having the far worse problem of tonic-clonic seizures.

Sometimes people with the type of epilepsy that causes them to have two different kinds of seizures will have to take two different medications, one to control each kind of seizure. In this case, too, they may have to simply learn to live with side effects caused by one or both medications.

For the most part, anticonvulsant medications work best on people who have idiopathic epilepsy (the kind for which there is no known cause), on people who don't have a lot of seizures, on people who begin taking a medication within less than a year after their first seizure, and on children whose seizures begin between the ages of two and five. As a result of taking a medication, about 58 percent of these people will never have another seizure, and the others will have no more than a few seizures during a lifetime, as long as they continue to take the medication. Generally, their doctors will want to check them with a blood examination about every three years to make sure that the dosage is still sufficient.

Is it annoying to have to always be sure to take two or three or more pills, capsules, or swallows of liquid every day forever? There are a great number of diseases and conditions besides epilepsy that require people to take medications all their lives—diabetes, high blood pressure, and others—and people who have to do this, soon get used to it. It becomes a habit, like brushing your teeth every morning or evening. However, there are some people who become overconfident when they don't have a seizure for a long time. They begin to feel that they're "cured," and stop taking their medication regularly or even cut it out entirely. This can be extremely dangerous. Doctors have found that suddenly stopping the use of an anticonvulsant drug, and sometimes even just not taking it regularly, can cause a sudden attack of the dreaded status epilepticus, the condition in which a person has seizure after seizure almost without pause, and which can cause death. This condition of course requires medical attention at once. Doctors treat status epilepticus by injecting Valium directly into the person's bloodstream so that it will get to the brain as quickly as possible. Valium, which is the kind of medication known as a tranquilizer, meaning "soothing" or "calming," is a lifesaver, because it can quickly bring a status epilepticus series of seizures to a halt.

However, while suddenly stopping the taking of a medication may cause serious trouble, doctors have found that *slowly* cutting down on medication until finally none at all is being taken, often seems to stop all further seizures for people with certain kinds of epilepsy. Many such people have never had another seizure. Of course, such a treatment must be done under the care and supervision of a doctor—a person with epilepsy should not try to do it alone.

In about 80 percent of all cases of epilepsy, seizures can be controlled by some kind of anticonvulsant medication. But, unfortunately, there are a number of persons for whom these medications just do not work well. For the most part these are people whose epilepsy was caused by a brain tumor, a stroke, a head injury, or a disease of the nervous system, such as meningitis. People whose seizures began before they were one year old or who have more than one kind of seizure are also difficult to help with medications. Doctors must try other kinds of treatments for these people.

In a few cases, surgery may be helpful. If doctors can locate the exact area of the brain where the seizures are being caused, and if the removal of that troublesome bit of brain tissue won't be the cause of any problems, such as loss of memory or inability to speak clearly, an operation may be performed to cut it away. Operations of this sort have helped some epileptic patients who could not be helped by taking medication. As is true of any kind of surgery, there is always a risk to the patient's life, and there is never any guarantee that the surgery will definitely help the patient as hoped—it doesn't always work. However, as time goes on, surgery is becoming much more successful because of constantly improving technology and new instruments, such as the gamma-ray scalpel.

A less drastic treatment that is helpful in a few cases for people who can't be helped by medication is a special diet known as a *ketogenic diet*. A ketone is a chemical compound, or mixture of certain chemical substances, that is manufactured in a person's body and is present in small amounts in everyone's bloodstream. It can act somewhat like a natural anticonvulsant medication and has a slight effect in preventing epileptic seizures. Eating a diet that is very high in fats and low in carbohydrates (sugars and starches) will raise the amount of ketones in a person's bloodstream, and of course this could be helpful if the person has epilepsy. However, a ketogenic diet consists mainly of vegetable oils and cream, which hardly makes up a satisfactory meal for anyone. It is generally used only for children with minor seizure problems that an anticonvulsant medication alone can't help.

There are a few other methods of treatment, but they are all mainly just experimental at this time and it's not at all certain that they will ever be of real value. One, known as "counterstimulation," is based on the fact that the stimulation, or "excitement," of the neurons causing an epileptic seizure can generally be stopped if the brain receives other stimulation in the right place. Some persons with epilepsy have been equipped with a

The battery-powered transmitter that is used in the "counterstimulation" treatment of epilepsy can be worn on a belt at the waist.

battery-powered transmitter that is worn on a belt at the waist and is connected, by means of wires that have been surgically implanted under the skin, to a set of electrodes surgically implanted in the cerebellum, the rearmost portion of the brain.

If a person feels an epileptic seizure coming on, he or she switches on the transmitter, which sends radio impulses into the cerebellum. The main job of the cerebellum is to filter out messages being sent from the cerebrum to the body's muscles, and when it is stimulated by the radio impulses from the transmitter it shuts down any large amount of electric discharge going on in the cerebrum and thus stops the epileptic seizure. While this method of preventing seizures has worked on some patients, there are a great many problems connected with it, and most doctors think it will never be as good a remedy as brain surgery.

Another experimental treatment makes use of the procedure known as biofeedback, in which a person checks his or her own brainwaves by means of a portable electroencephalograph and uses deep-breathing, relaxation, and other techniques to try to actually control the brain's activity. This has helped a few of those with epilepsy who couldn't be helped in any other way, but it is extremely difficult to do.

For the most part, most people with epilepsy depend mainly upon anticonvulsant drugs and simply adjust their lives around the fact that they may, at any time, have a seizure. This means taking a great many precautions. In general, the person has to try to exercise regularly, get regular and plentiful sleep, eat a well-

One experimental method of treating epilepsy is through biofeedback, in which through the use of an electroencephalograph of a person is able to monitor his or her own brain waves, and use deep-breathing, relaxation, and other techniques to try to control the brain's activity.

balanced diet, avoid stress as much as possible, and avoid drinking a lot of alcoholic drinks. Too much alcohol can bring on a seizure. So could the use of abusive drugs, which should be avoided by everyone in any case, of course. People with epilepsy also have to avoid putting themselves into situations where they might be injured or even killed if they were to have a seizure. For example, many of those who face the risk of a tonic-clonic seizure take only showers and never baths, because they could easily drown in bathwater if they became unconscious in the tub. They avoid climbing a ladder, because if they had a seizure and fell off, they could be seriously injured. Some persons with epilepsy learn to sleep without pillows because if they were to have a seizure that caused them to push their face into the pillow, they could suffocate. Those who like to swim must always have someone with them who could help if they should have a seizure while in the water.

Many of those with epilepsy are also affected by the fact that a great many people still have old-fashioned odd ideas about epilepsy, and look down on persons with epilepsy as being "retarded," "abnormal," and generally just "different" enough so as to be unacceptable. Especially for a teenager who has epilepsy, it can be a crushing, shattering thing to know that some other teenagers think of you that way!

And so, it is to be hoped that just as great new strides are being made in doctors' understanding and treatment of epilepsy, great new strides will be made in finally getting rid of all the silly old-fashioned ideas that many people have about epilepsy, and in helping everyone understand what epilepsy really is. If you know a person with epilepsy or if you ever meet one—which you almost certainly will, sometime—remember that that person is *just like you,* except that he or she has something wrong with a part of the body that might, at any time, bring about unconsciousness for a few minutes or some other type of attack that might result in odd behavior for a little while. But people with epilepsy are no danger to you in any way, they don't have to be "treated with kid gloves," and they might turn out to be the best of friends!

CHAPTER

7

WHAT TO DO IF SOMEONE YOU KNOW HAS AN EPILEPTIC SEIZURE

If it is a grand mal, or tonic-clonic, seizure, in which the person falls to the ground unconscious, with jerking arms and legs—

Don't panic. Even though the person may have made a screaming sound, and even though his or her face may be contorted as if with pain, remember that the person is unconscious and is not actually in any pain. The seizure will probably run its course without causing any major harm.

If there are any sharp objects on the ground or floor where the person has fallen, quickly clear them away so that the person won't get gashed or cut.

If possible, loosen the clothing around the person's neck.

DO NOT *put anything into the person's mouth to try to prevent him or her from biting or swallowing the tongue. You would probably be too late to prevent the biting of the tongue because that usually would happen at about the instant the attack begins. As for swallowing the tongue, this never actually happens. But putting something into the person's mouth can cause an injury to the teeth or throat.*

As the person's body relaxes and the muscle stiffness ends, gently turn the person's head to one side to help keep him or her from possibly choking on saliva.

Normally, a tonic-clonic seizure will be over in about fifteen to twenty minutes. If it lasts longer than this, or if a new seizure seems to be starting, the person may be having status epilepticus seizures and needs immediate medical attention. Telephone for paramedics or for an ambulance to take the person to the emergency ward of a hospital, or for whatever can be done to get the help needed.

If it is a petit mal, or absence, seizure, in which the person is staring blankly into space and appears to be frozen in movement—

Do nothing. The seizure will be over in a few seconds with no harm to the person.

If it is a partial, or psychomotor, seizure, in which the person is behaving oddly, pulling at his or her clothing, muttering the same words over and over, etc.—

The person having the seizure may begin to walk or even run, aimlessly. Stay near, but unless he or she is about to do something dangerous, such as wander out into heavy traffic or walk off the edge of a high place, do not interfere. Interference could cause the person to try to resist you and cause injury—either to the person or to you. In general, just let the seizure take its course until it comes to an end.

For further information about epilepsy, and assistance if necessary, contact the Epilepsy Foundation of America, a nonprofit, charitable organization dedicated to the welfare of people with epilepsy. Call, toll-free, 1-800-EFA-1000, or write to the Office of Public Relations, Epilepsy Foundation of America, 4351 Garden City Drive, Landover MD 20785.

GLOSSARY

Absence seizure. The type of seizure in which the affected person loses consciousness and muscular control for only a few seconds, without falling or becoming stiff. Formerly known as *petit mal.*

Arteries. The blood vessels that carry the blood from the heart to all parts of the body.

Arteriosclerosis. A condition in which a person's arteries have become filled with a fatty or chalklike substance that makes them harder and thicker, making it difficult for the blood to flow through easily.

Atonic seizure. The type of seizure in which the affected person momentarily loses control of the muscles and falls down. Also called a "drop seizure."

Aura. The name given to the sensation somewhat like a cool breeze flowing through the body, that many persons with epilepsy feel just before a seizure.

Autonomic seizure. A type of seizure in which the affected person may suffer a series of headaches or stomachaches, or prolonged nausea or fever, which is not typical of other types of seizures.

(85)

Axon. The long, stemlike portion of a nerve cell, which carries the nerve impulses out of the main body of the cell.

Brain stem. The bottom, stalklike part of the brain, which connects to the spinal cord.

CAT scan. A process in which a picture of an internal part of a person's body is made by a combination of x ray and computer. X rays make many cross-section views of the body part, and the computer fits all these sections together to form a picture of the whole part on a television screen.

Central nervous system. The brain and spinal cord.

Cerebellum. An orange-sized part of the brain at the bottom and slightly to the rear of the main part.

Cerebrum. The main, front part of the brain, which makes up about 85 percent of the whole brain.

Cro-Magnons. The name given to the earliest-known members of the present-day human race, who lived about thirty-thousand years ago.

Dendrites. The branchlike parts of a nerve cell, which receive the impulses from other cells.

Electrocardiogram. A chart of the action of a person's heart, made by converting the heartbeats to electrical impulses that cause an ink-filled pen to make a continuous mark on an unrolling sheet of paper.

Electroencephalograph. A machine that records the electrical activity of a person's brain.

Epilepsy, idiopathic. The form of epilepsy for which there is no known cause.

Epilepsy, symptomatic. The form of epilepsy for which there is a known cause, such as a scar on the brain.

Grand mal seizure. See *Tonic-clonic seizure.*

Ketogenic diet. A high-fat, low-carbohydrate diet that causes the body to produce more of the chemical compounds known as ketones, which are helpful in preventing epileptic seizures.

Medication. A mixture of chemicals or biological substances in pill, capsule, or liquid form, that are given by mouth or injection to cure or control an illness or health problem. Medications for epilepsy help prevent seizures.

Motor seizure. The type of seizure that generally begins with a sharp tingling in one hand, which moves up the arm and sometimes down a leg on the same side of the body.

Myoclonic seizure. The type of seizure in which the affected person suffers such violent muscular jerks that he or she may be thrown to the ground or may hurl away any object they are holding.

Neurons. Nerve cells.

Nucleus. A mass of special material at the center of most plant and animal cells. It consists of a complicated arrangement of proteins, acids, and fats, and controls the growth, health, and other functions of the cell.

Petit mal seizure. See *Absence seizure.*

Psychomotor seizure. The type of seizure that affects a person's awareness and actions. Persons having this kind of seizure often wander about, pull at their clothing, etc.

Receptors. Special types of nerve cells that are sensitive to a form of stimulation such as the action of sound waves, light waves, heat, etc.

Sensory seizure. The type of seizure in which the affected person may see or hear sights or sounds that are not actually present.

Tonic-clonic seizures. The type of seizure in which the affected person loses consciousness and muscular control, falling to the ground and becoming stiff. Formerly called *grand mal.*

Status epilepticus. A condition in which a person with epilepsy has a series of seizures, one after another, with no pause in between.

BIBLIOGRAPHY

Burden, George, and Schurr, Peter. *Understanding Epilepsy.* Woodstock, NY: Beekman Books, 1976.

Hazeldine, Peter. *Epilepsy: What Is It, What Causes It and Advice on its Successful Management.* England: Sterling, 1986.

Hermes, Patricia. *What If They Knew?* New York: Harcourt Brace Jovanovich, 1980.

Hopkins, Anthony. *Epilepsy: The Facts.* New York: Oxford University Press, 1981.

Schneider, Joseph W., and Conrad, Peter. *Having Epilepsy: The Experience & Control of Illness.* Philadelphia: Temple University Press, 1985.

Silverstein, Alvin and Virginia B. *Epilepsy.* New York: Harper & Row Junior Books, 1974.

Temkin, Owsei. *The Falling Sickness: A History of Epilepsy from the Greeks to the Beginnings of Modern Neurology,* 2nd rev. ed. Charlotte, NC: UMI Publications, 1970.

INDEX

Page numbers in *italics* refer to illustrations.

Absence seizures, 45, 46, 48, 49, 70, 82
Age, 17, 52, 53, 56, 57, 60, 79
Alcohol, 79
Alexander the Great, 14, 22
Ancient times, epilepsy in, 14, 22–25
Animals:
    brains of, 39
    with epilepsy, 17
Anticonvulsant drugs, 69–74, 77
Arteries, hardening of, 17
Arteriosclerosis, 53, *55*, 56
Athletes, 16

Atonic seizures, 45–46
Aura, 24, 25, 61
Autonomic seizures, 47
Axon, 40, 42

Beddoes, Thomas, 29
Berger, Dr. Johannes, 33
Biofeedback, 77, *78*
Blood tests, 62, 71, 73
Brain, 13, 37
    CAT scans of, *54*, 62, *63*
    composition and functions of, 37–49
    epilepsy as disease of, 13, 14, 23, 25, 38, 31, 33, 37–49, 51–56, 64, 69–70, 75
    injury to, 49, 52–56
    permanent disorder, 17
    scars, 56–57

Brain (continued)
    surgery, 74–75, 77
    tumors, 17, 53, 54, 60,
        62, 74
Brain stem, 39
Breughel, Pieter, 26
Bromide of potassium, 30–31,
    33

Caesar, Julius, 14, 15, 23
CAT scans, 54, 62, 63
Causes of epilepsy, 17, 49, 51–
    58, 74
Cells, 37, 40, 42, 58
Cerebellum, 39, 40, 77
Cerebrum, 39, 40, 45
Chemical disturbances, 56
Chemical reactions, 42, 57
Childhood epilepsy, 17, 52,
    59–60, 72–73, 75
Counterstimulation, 75, 76, 77
Crime, 34
Cro-Magnons, 21
Cure for epilepsy, lack of, 18

Deafness, 14
Death, 17, 18, 73
"Demonic disease," epilepsy
    as, 25
Dendrites, 40, 42
Depakene, 70, 71, 72
Diabetes, 73
Diagnosis of epilepsy, 59–67
Diet, 23, 28, 77, 79
    ketogenic, 75
Dilantin, 70, 71, 72
Discrimination against epilep-
    tics, 34
Dostoevski, Fyodor, 16

Electrical charges in the brain,
    42, 43, 46, 64, 65–66, 77
Electrocardiogram, 62

Electroencephalogram (EEG),
    64, 65–66, 67
Electroencephalograph, 33, 64,
    65–66, 67, 77, 78
Employment, 34
Encephalitis, 56
Epilepsy:
    causes of, 17, 49, 51–58,
        74
    and death, 17, 18, 73
    definition of, 13, 14
    diagnosis of, 59–67
    as disease of the brain, 13,
        14, 23, 25, 28, 31, 33,
        37–49, 51–56, 64, 69–
        70, 75
    early remedies for, 22, 23,
        25, 26, 27–28, 29–31,
        32, 33
    famous people with, 14,
        15, 16
    history of, 21–35
    idiopathic, 51, 57–58, 72
    kinds of seizures, 13–14,
        18, 19, 30, 44–49, 70
    superstitions about, 22,
        23, 25, 26, 27, 28, 29–
        30, 33–34
    symptomatic, 51–57
    timing of seizures, 13, 27,
        30
    treatment of, 18, 19, 69–
        80
    warning symptoms of, 23–
        25
    what to do around, 81–83
Epileptic state, 18, 73–74, 82
Europe, history of epilepsy in,
    22–33
Exercise, 77

Fainting spells, 13, 45, 47, 59,
    60, 61, 81

"Falling sickness," epilepsy as, 23

Famous people with epilepsy, 14, *15*, 16

Ferdinandus, 27

Fevers, 47, 60

France, 16

Frequency of epilepsy, 17

Galen, 23, *24*

Gamma-ray scalpel, 75

General seizures, 48

German measles, 52

Germany, 25, 29

Glia, 37

Grand mal seizures, 44, 81

Gray matter, 39

Greece, ancient, 14, 22–23, 25

Handel, George Frederick, *15*, 16

Hauptmann, Alfred, 33

Headaches, 45, 47

Head injuries, 17, 53, 56, 74

Hearing, sense of, 38, 39, 47

Heart trouble, 60, 62

Heredity, 34, 58

High blood pressure, 73

Hippocrates, 22–23

History of epilepsy, 21–35

Howatt, Gary, 16

Hypoglycemia, 60, 62

Idiopathic epilepsy, 51, 57–58, 72

Infections, 48, 60

Infectious disease, 52, 54, 74

Information about epilepsy, 83

Intelligence, 49

Jackson, Dr. Hughlings, 31

Ketogenic diet, 75

Kinds of seizures, 13–14, 18, 19, 30, 44–49, 70

Lazzeri, Tony, 16

Life insurance, 34

Liver, 70

Lobes, 40, 46

Locock, Sir Charles, 30–31

London, 30

Luther, Martin, 25

Macedonia, 14

Magical folklore remedies, 22, 23, 25, *26*, 27–28, 29, 34

Mammals, 17

Marek, Jan, 28

Measles, 52

Medications, 18, 19, 31, 33, 34

  anticonvulsant, 69–74, 77

  bromide of potassium, 30–31, 33

  choice of, 70–72

  discontinued use of, 73–74

  overuse of, 48

  phenobarbital, 33

  side effects of, 71, 72

Memory, 15

Meningitis, 52, 56, 62, 74

Mental institutions, 29, 31, *32*, 33

Middle Ages, 25–28

Moon, epilepsy "caused" by, 27, 30

Moreau, 30

Motor cortex, 40, 44

Motor seizures, 47, 48

Muscle stiffness, 44, 46, 81, 82

Myoclinic seizures, 46

Napoleon Bonaparte, *15*, 16

Near East, history of epilepsy in, 22, 28
Nervous system, 17, 38, 39, 40, 47, 51
Neurons, 37, 39, 40–43, 45, 46, 47, 48, 57, 70, 75

Older people, epilepsy in, 17, 53, 56, 60

Partial seizures, 48, 82
Personality disorders, 33
Petit mal seizures. See Absence seizures
Phenobarbital, 33
Physical examination, 61–62, 67
Pius IX, Pope, 16
Poisoning, 56
Prehistoric people with epilepsy, 21
Psychomotor seizures, 46–47, 48, 49, 82

Radiation, 52
Receptors, 39
Religion, 27
Rome, ancient, 23, 24, 25
Royal Medical and Chirurgical Society (London), 30

Scars, brain, 56–57
Senses, 38, 39, 46, 47
Sensory seizures, 47, 48
Side effects of medications, 71, 72
Sight, sense of, 38, 39, 47
Sleep, 77, 79
    lack of, 48
Smell, sense of, 38, 39, 46
Spinal cord, 39
Status epilepticus, 18, 73–74, 82

Stomachaches, 47
Strokes, 17, 56, 62, 74
Superstitions about epilepsy, 22, 23, 25, 26, 27, 28, 29–30, 33–34
Surgery, 74–75, 77
Swimming, 79
Symptomatic epilepsy, 51–57

Taste, sense of, 38, 39, 46
Timing of seizures, 13, 27, 30
Tissot, 29
Tongue biting, 82
Tonic-clonic seizures, 45, 46, 48, 49, 70, 72, 79, 81, 82
Treatment, 18, 19, 69–80
    biofeedback, 77, 78
    counterstimulation, 75, 76, 77
    diet, 75
    drugs, 30–31, 33, 69–74, 77
    history of, 21–35
    magical folklore, 22, 23, 25, 26, 27–28, 29, 34
    surgery, 74–75, 77
Tuberculosis, 52
Tumors, brain, 17, 53, 54, 60, 62, 74

Unconsciousness, 45, 47, 59, 60, 61, 81

Valentine, Saint, 25, 27
Valium, 73–74
Van Gogh, Vincent, 15, 16

Warning symptoms of epilepsy, 23–25
Wilks, Dr. Samuel, 31

Zarontin, 70, 71